THINK ABOUT THIS

THINGS THAT ARE SURELY GOING TO OPEN YOUR EYES.

MAHIR BUKSH

This book is yet again dedicated to a really special person that I cannot name.

This person is just special in everything that they do and I

fully believe that they always will be.

Dedicating this specefically to her smile, her kindness and her everything.

If you're reading this, then know that YOU are the hope that yet again pushed me to write this.

Thank you for existing.

Contents

Preface

As I grew older, I learned and realised so many things. Some of them being in this book in one way or the other. But with growth comes heartbreaks, consequences and certain things that this world believes and in those things, I found fractures. Cracks that were visible but covered with the intangible bandages that some of use don't even realise exist. My main focus is those fractures, along with some beautiful things so things are not all dark. Hope this book becomes your food for thought.

Happy reading!

The unusual theory of Happiness

Humans are weird. Always either they are asking questions around happiness like- "How have you been?" and their companions being responsive with words like "yeah man, all good!" with the 'good' implying that they are in most cases averagely satisfied with their life. There are a plethora of humans around the world, and most prominently around you. Humans, who are chasing this Idea of happiness as if it were a dog that ran away or a cab that they have to catch. Contrary to this, there are also people who are a different breed altogether. These are also the ones that I understand to a certain extent. The ones that portray the idea that happiness is not outside, but rather an inside job. The idea that you generate your own happiness from your unique thoughts, and actions. There are also a third type of people that I encounter. I see the people dressed in the most epitomes of dresses and clothes and it radiates the idea that they are happy with this choice of clothes they selected. But then, "Mahir, how come you do not like these clothes and why are you so disinterested!?" my mother tells me. I do not understand how someone or most people choosing a single way of channeling happiness in the form of clothes defines the way of "everyone's" happiness. There's a breed of people who are at most times, disinterested. They are not necessarily disinterested in the idea of happiness, but rather in the methods of it. Methods to channel or define happiness that have been so overly used by most of society's population that they according to some, are the "only" ways to be happy. But there is growth in society. People seem to follow more and more in the leads of the second kind of people who define happiness as internal. This has convinced of people and a massive number of them already have ingrained the idea of happiness being present within themselves and live by it every day. They have created quotes like "you only live once" and "where fear ends, life begins" and so many more in their defense to justify their idea of happiness. Nothing wrong with that, but this still does not resolve the issue. The issue that people from the first breed of population seem to be having with the third breed of population. People seem to be putting immaculous efforts in making the society a happier place, yet fail to put enough efforts in understanding the lesser percentage of population who they have seemingly termed as "weird". The people from the "weird" population at times seem to enjoy most things that other people may not find at all interesting like- choosing comfortable and lousy clothes instead of tight and vibrant ones, or choosing a same old bland home dish they ate yesterday instead of a fancy restaurant dish but somehow the idea that these things seem to be noticeably be interesting to some of us people is not sold amongst the larger population. There is also this phrase that I came across – "to live and let live" as formed by some of the assumed people of the lesser percentage of people. Phrases like this were invented in defense to their own safety and happiness because the people of the larger population find it rather difficult to leave other people in the way that they feel happy. There's also this really weird phenomena around happiness. The phenomena that there ARE different kinds of happiness. There is happiness generated through and within oneself, which is different from the happiness given by an external object. Then there is also the happiness that comes from romantic love. The feeling of elation and a host of feel-good emotions that allow you to elevate your happiness without even trying up until levels you didn't even know existed. The burst of "emotional high" that you feel in your very bones when the person your heart chose, smiles. Their well being and safety brings about a new meaning to what happiness means for you. There is on the contrary, also the happiness you feel after your significant other and you no longer find happiness in each other and therefore decide to go on your own journeys to find happiness. This sense of freedom after you have taken back the power of happiness in your own hands brings about a new fresh breath of rejuvenating happiness. This experience to now do everything by your own self, with your hands and for your very own self. This brings about a different kind of happiness all together. People are all sorts of unique. Some people use a plethora of substances to trigger happiness. Using tobaccos and the finest of wines are among the few things that people trick their brain with to trigger the biological chemicals of happiness. Knowing this leads to their downfall, they refuse to stop and continue to be "happy" in their own way. But then, am I now not sounding like the bigger percentage of the population while trying to defend the lesser half of the population? Oh, how ironical! But I ask, when will we see the day that people are happy with not just themselves but also with the other people they call "weird"? I guess it will all come with acceptance.

Indian women and...tradition?

It is not as much of a matter of keeping it suppressed as much as it is of accepting and victimizing to women to this hollow structure. I hear my elders say how the same thing that is acceptable and even appreciating for me is rather shunned by heavy words for my little sisters. “How would she do it son? Our elders do not allow it and neither does our ‘beliefs’.” You see your mother everyday and see her do nothing but the household work that is “expected” of her. I ask, why her? The deeper disappoint lies in the fact that as two children grow up, a brother and a sister, they at some level are given different privileges and given access to even the good things in life in different quantities. Quantities that are considered “safe” for the sister, and “not necessary” for the brother. This is far a deeper wound in the most traditional houses. Homes of the mothers and sisters and aunts who were denied access to education or were told to focus more on the household work that will be “necessary and expected of her” once married. I feel pity when I ask my mother. “Mamma, what did you wanted to become when you were not thinking about marriage?” “son, I wanted a better life for myself”. She says after a long pause to my question, not knowing or remembering what did she want for herself. Years of conditioning by her own mother who received little to no education despite showing a vast intellect in the most complicated of household matters breaks my heart. It breaks because women have been oppressed so much so that the ones who had no one to fight for them and no one to guide their voice ended up shunning themselves and suppressing their most heartfelt desires because they assumed that victimization is what keeps us safe from "society". This victimization made a home in all of their hearts, making them forget that life only happens once. My grandmother never answered the question to what her life purpose is. She did not understand the question. I guess I was asking her what she truly looked like, what was her soul like. But patriarchy has unknowingly killed that part of her and even when I tried my best looking for her, I simply couldn't find her. The answer to my life purpose question did bring something up though. She says "To take care of all of you and before that, to take care of your mother." As I see my mother, who works tirelessly throughout half the day and then rests the other half and night, some of our conversations do include me asking how she would like to spend the rest of her day, to which she is only able to express her pain that passes through her everyday due to long hours of work. She is mostly left with no energy to spend her day any other ways except resting. Hanging on Papa for monetary support, she at times breaks and is unable to process her frustration when there is a quarrel and her only source of money for herself is gone for awhile. I ask, is my mother and yours destined to work tirelessly every day until one day death comes for them? Is this their only purpose in life? To serve us day in and day out and only earn rest in return? Have we, as the second largest population reduced our women to mere work-maids in the name of old traditions? Now I may be very well called a feminist here but all I am trying is to state some little facts. Facts that may feel repeated, Ideas that may seem unoriginal but! I ask you to think. Go ahead and ask your families as to why cannot your sister go out partying all night when you as her brother can. Why doesn't your mother remember her dreams? Why does she veil herself in silence on the questions of HER happiness and all her replies only include your well being and comfort, even if it means sacrificing her own? I am not against tradition but am openly against the practice of victimization in the name of "tradition". Maybe we all have hopes that someday it will all be better, but I ask how? How would and most importantly who would gather the courage to break our women out of the shackles of belittlement in the name of "safety". Now I agree that the world is changing and all the good things that women are now able to enjoy but as long as we as a population refuse to introspect, the root of this evil will continue to be passed onto generations. Children that see the men in their house mistreat women and women who find comfort in victimization to avoid going against the society will continue to pass on wildfires of patriarchy in all the generations to come. Perhaps we could start, perhaps. To trust our Betees and Bahus that with changing times, they can look after themselves and would call their 'men' when absolutely necessary. To trust them that yes, they too are born as intelligent. Not the same as their brother or father, but as themselves and when will we find acceptance in the fact that our grandmothers have the same social intellect as our grandfathers. And as we learn acceptance, we will push hard for our Bahus and Betees for they too deserve a

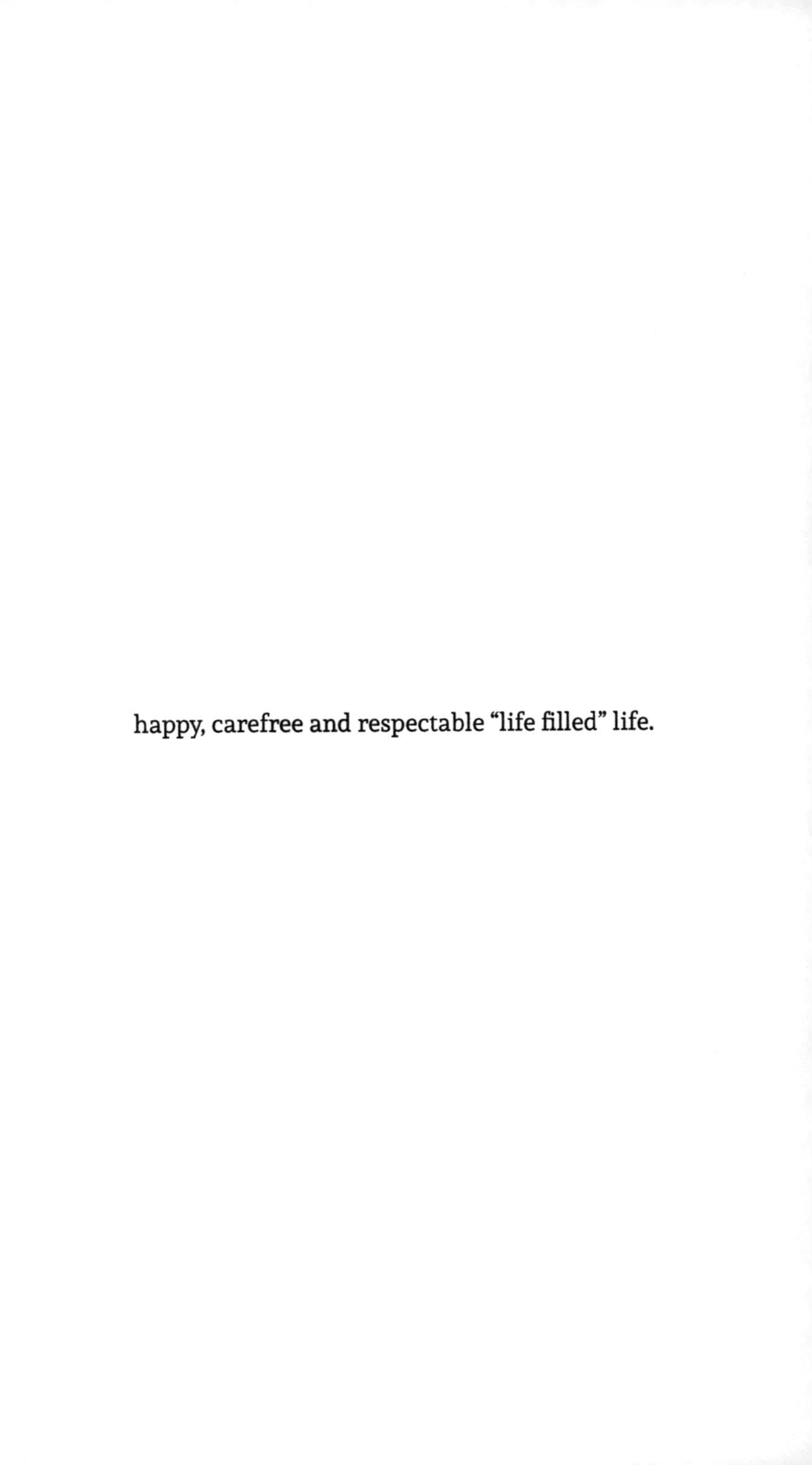

happy, carefree and respectable “life filled” life.

Animals: friends or food?

If not all of us, certainly most of us love animals and I am to be honest, quite "drunk in love" when I see them around me. I mean, is there a reason to not love them? They are just your average human child but much cuter. They have colorful furs, small cute faces and paws and wandering eyes and the best part? They remain children even if they have had years of life under their skin. A cat of 10 year old will still play like a child of human at the age of five. They cross cones, jump obstacles and fight water all because? They are innocent. Innocent in the ways that human can never be. They understand love and happy time and food and treats and that is all. They also understand pain. They see you cry and they come and try to snuggle with you, comforting you in the only way that they know. This tells you that they have a soul, but wait. Do they? I see colleagues I know discuss with me about how they like their chicken biryani and kebabs and how they like it spicy or salty but I never see someone who stops by my house to tell me that they have stopped eating meat because it is wrong. I see people getting aggressive and overly enthusiastic over something that hurts their fragile egos or even their innocent families but never once have I encountered someone getting furious over a meat shop and taking not aggressive, but proper actions to stop them. Ok, let us hypothetically agree that killing certain animals for food is God's way but what about humans proceeding to cats and dogs? Crickets? Snails? Are they also "food from God"? And what about the fact that when an animal is being harassed on the street when you are working from home or in the way to your office and you see a mother dog protecting her babies from human "children" cooing and encircling her but you decide that you are late or busy and pass by without notice, or more accurately – in ignorance. Tell me you did not see an animal being harassed while you were in close quarters. How does your heart not wrench in excruciating frustration and anger when you see someone who is a mother who has no one to look after her and no one but herself to defend herself? How do you not consider the fact that someone who has to fight on a day to day basis for basic amenities like food and water will now have to fight harder because despite you being educated and capable, decided to ignore their cry for help as if they were not "worth your time". Slaughter houses run and so do Poultry farms. Chickens, goats, cows and even fur factories that are run by the most indignant and heartless of humans and as we take a moment to decide that we will eat pork tomorrow, we let a small taste of the tongue to start a chain reaction of events that ends in a another innocent life taking its last few breaths for one last night before being put to death to serve the pleasure on our tongues the next morning. People are good, they still are yes. But when will there come a day when a female dog will be able to safely leave its children behind with human children to play with without the fear that they may be killed after she leaves. They cry, and we turn our ears as if made of stone to avoid getting in trouble. I will say that however blessed I am, I am a tad bit disappointed and infuriated at the cowardice of people I know to stop me from saving the poor souls because according to them I will be called "a madman by society for fighting for animals". When will chickens eat natural food that allows them to flourish and not artificial food that only helps them get fatter and fatter which will be needed for them to "taste" better? When will goats and cows and pigs live fuller and longer lives? Yes, it will be hard because not just in India, but all around the world, people have come to believe the idea that certain animals is equivalent to just food and we cannot leave them and their population would proliferate out of control and what not, but ask this – to control their population your sole reason to kill them so mercilessly? There are for sure a hundred other ways that they can reproduce at a slower rate, isn't there? Then why would you constantly allow yourself to live in denial? In denial of the fact that you turn a blind eye when you see a lesser cute version of your pet scrounging desperately for food in the streets. Why do you turn a deaf ear to the cries of puppies that are being harassed by your very own street boys? When will animals come out of their hidden places and feel safe? As a child born in India, I remember reading and looking at multiple illustrations in culture of how the cows and peacocks and goats and literally all animals alike prospered in the time when Lord Krishna walked the earth. His flute tempted peacocks to lend him their feathers and not just him, the humans and shepherds that lived at that time not just respected, but loved their animals with all of their hearts. A calf born to their cow was treated with the same care as was a new born in their house. Did we, over the years, really let our souls corrupt to this poisonous level? I hear wise men say

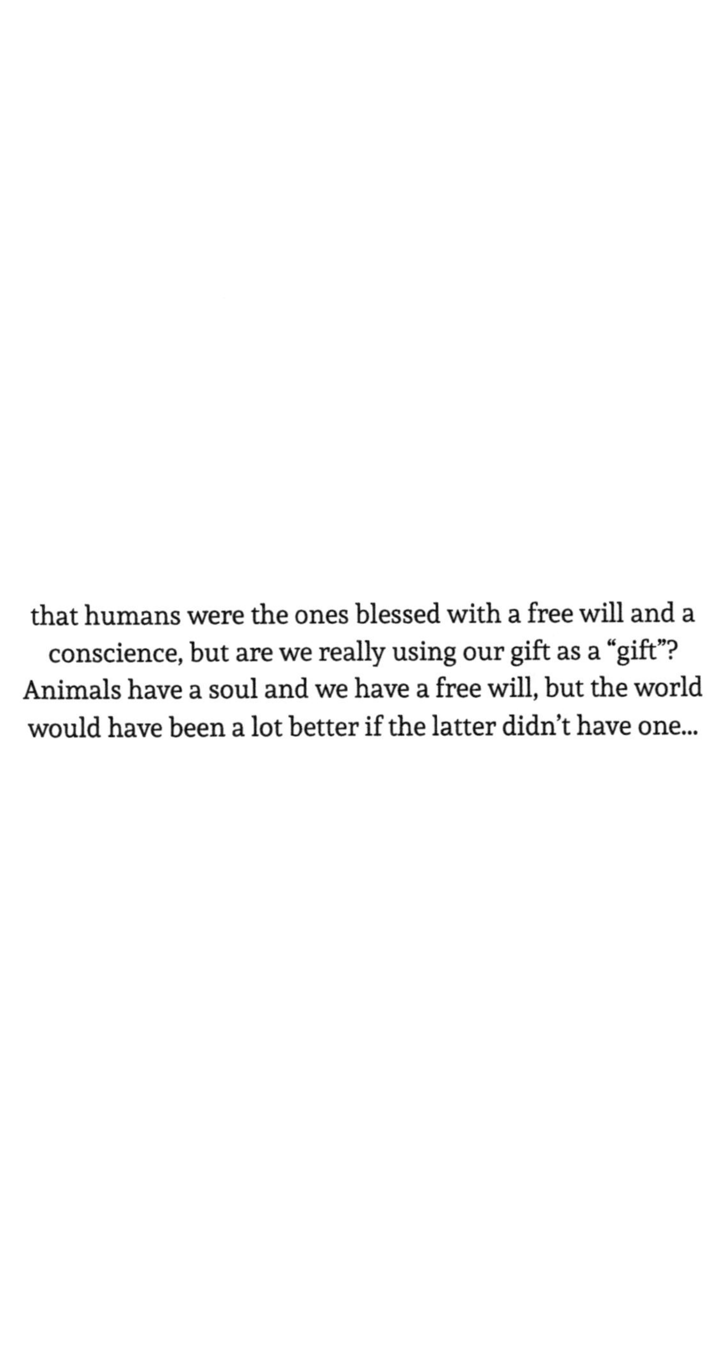

that humans were the ones blessed with a free will and a conscience, but are we really using our gift as a "gift"? Animals have a soul and we have a free will, but the world would have been a lot better if the latter didn't have one...

Fate? or free will?

Humans live all of their lives believing in the power of free will and its additional advantages. The sense of control! Ah, what a pleasure! We can sleep whenever we like, laugh at something that others may not find hilarious and reshape our bodies in the most exquisite of ways imaginable. But tell me, if we control our lives or more specifically our "fates" then why do we hear elders and wiser people saying that you meet your death right where you were fated to? If we have the power to change future outcomes and to an extent even our fates, then why do we meet death and avoid it even the way it is "written"? How can anything that is independent of attached outcomes be still attached to only a specific outcome despite us making a hundred choices that will for sure avoid it? I ask you – look at a person who is only mildly mentally ill. They understand work life and that it brings money which makes life better but they are unable to understand the depth that work-life demands and therefore they fail to do it altogether. Or for instance, They are interpreted as "ill of mind" by the people they live with and every time they 'try' to work, they are tricked by their own people to not take a chance at work altogether because they are not "fit in the mind". What is at play here? Is it fate that tells us that this specific human is supposed to sit on their couch for the rest of their lives until death meets them, therefore living a life without purpose? Or is it free will of or the misuse of it on the part of the people that love them that would again end in their life being manipulated to be lived purposeless? Life brings with it the many, many instances that are sometimes the living proof that "some things" and "some ones" are written in the stars but then again I fail to understand that humans still believe in the lives they live being free willed. The confusion is so much so that it makes you question that if free will or fate exists separately or are they a work in mesh, working alongside each other to make each of us live a unique life. There are instances when free will is seen skillfully at work like for example a simple child of fifteen choosing commerce instead of science as his subject for future studies despite him being pressured by everyone to choose medical sciences and give in to the "doctors-are-the-best-earners" syndrome. The child refuses to break under the pressure and listens to his heart instead, which grows in fascination at how multi millionaires start businesses that solve the needs of so many people around the world. He makes a conscious decision to "choose" it, putting his conscience and more specifically – free will at work. If you were to take another example, the one made in love where two people "accidently" meet "by chance" and decide through a series of events that these two individuals would bring out the best in each other if they stay together. They are fated "as a match made in heaven". Now, again what is at play here? Was it fate that was pre-decided and made them meet up through so many consequences that brought them together? Or was it the free will of these individuals that allowed them to make many many conscious choices that lead them here? Humans have a plenty amount of questions that need answering or deserve explanations but are just unanswerable or do not have an explanation and yes, we could alternatively find satisfaction in the facts stated above as mere "increment of knowledge and information". But however we see it, there is more to both fate and free will. It is a fact that maybe in some context the both of them working together simultaneously can be believed but some things just are more than simple explanations. Some things defy all logic that revolves around fate and free will alike and deserve an explanation but have been unable to earn the privilege. But despite all things at hand, it is safe to believe the sentence that it is perhaps fate that is written with the very strings of every outcome that we can think of and entangling each of them to the most singular of experiences by all means until it results in our deaths. Fate indeed is the very collection of all of our free will making us believe only the illusion that we are in control when in all reality; it is fate itself that has been pulling the strings since forever.

Adult stars and "the land of tradition".

Living in the twenty first century, we all of us are very "open" and there's nothing that is hidden from anyone. Most people, especially a person of the general population would very well be aware of and know of someone who is a known celebrity or a person of high status. Among many individuals come - adult stars. The faces, well some of them, are prominently quite known by most of the current population, especially youngsters. The most famous of adult stars are as popular as your average Hollywood actor or actress. Their professions are mostly same with both parties "acting" for conveying a form of entertainment and there is nothing wrong with it. Both the parties seem to be ever increasing, with the industries bringing more and more talented people into the mix. Certain percentage of the "traditional" population however, seem to find in it, immorality. A good chunk of the population seems to be frustrated and equally angered at the latter industry. Since the latter industry takes its roots and operates inside United States for the most part, there is still some, even if little, comfort that at least this "thing" is away from their children. The fact that the western culture is amusingly comfortable in their children leaving homes to live their lives independently however they wish is known to most percentage of the current "traditional" generation. Things like an "Onlyfans" are becoming increasingly common with even the most popular of people talking about it being a good option with an open mind. But let us shift a little bit of attention here. If a woman of consenting age were to decide opening an adult page for herself, not for money, but because she feels comfortable in her own skin and feels good to celebrate herself with the world, there would be judgment. Women all around the world, from all backgrounds are all alike. They all have beautiful hearts. Hearts that are unique to each of them and every heart yearns for something that is personal and thrilling even to themselves, so why I ask, are there no roots of someplace where there is freedom? Freedom to choose a life that is true to themselves and not "society"? The sad orthodox thinking in the "land of tradition" is relatively high and still prevails. And yes we all know the ever surrounding beliefs that "women are supposed to veil themselves" or "women are not supposed to make certain choices for themselves" but is this what still prevails? When will be there a day when we celebrate not just women but all the choices that all the people make for themselves with their own heart? How is certainly not the battle, because the world has vastly advanced in all the many "how to's". There are plenty of blogs out there. The battle, along with the question, is when. I look forward to a day when along with other things beautiful, may we learn to celebrate and be understanding of choices. However they may be made by anyone whatsoever. May we support them with love. With kindness. May we come to terms with the fact that certain things that may not make us happy, do make some people the happiest and may we offer smiles and not judgments.

Life and other little things.

Trust in time, for in time you will find the cure. The willingness to let go. To go towards something beautiful and to get away from something darker.

Even if they do not deserve it, Even if they are unkind or are not very close to your soul, Even if they may not understand or are not capable enough to handle it, you owe it to your own soul to try. Try it to the point where the horizon of your mind's eye is able to see. You owe it not to them, but to the humanity in you. To the love that lives in you. You owe your best to try.

The reason two people engage in physical or mental violence is not always out of ferocity or jealousy, but to see it at the very root, they do indulge in it because a right opinion or belief in one's own self clashes or is different from the opinion or belief in the other person's self and they assume that there is not enough place for two contradicting beliefs in this singular world.

The heart knows. You may believe that you can use your the wits of your mind to trick it, but trust me. It knows. There are instances where you may be able to fully believe your own lie that you know in your heart is not right, but eventually the truth catches on and oh! how it shatters your very soul.

Size does matter but not in the way you think. It does not matter in the physical ways. Several people over the centuries have stood as the evidence to it. Then what do I mean by size? The size of your thoughts. It is the only size that matters.

It is concluded that with enough evidence and with enough confidence, you can make people belief anything and everything. No matter how big or small the thought. If it can be paired with just enough actions, your thought becomes a reality in the eyes of those who surround you.

Why isn't love the answer? Why isn't it enough? If two people are apart and still care about each other, isn't love the only thing holding them together? If two lifelong rivals kill one of the other, wouldn't love concealed as honor, bring the one alive to the others death? I ask, if love is the last thread that binds people in the end times, then why isn't enough to make people stay until end times?

It is not the stories that we like. Stories are just words to be heard, mere alphabets flowing from one ring to the next. It is the touch of victory, the taste of defeat and the sweetness of love that make us immerse in it, producing a feeling of liking it.

Lessons are nothing to be learned, that I have come to fully realize. They are a thing to be happened to us, to help us bloom. This, I have come to accept.

You will be young and you will be stupid. You will immerse yourself in the utmost blasphemous of acts and you will want to never stop, so keep going. Because then you will be hurt, and you will be loved, and you will fall and you will become what people call wisdom.

Hate is all around us. Always has been. It is one of the prime ingredients of the famous seven sins, but why is it so? Why is someone different being belittled and shamed just because their thoughts are different? What is the cause behind some people just being shunned when their only crime is their voice?

How do hearts break? I ask, having gone through quite a many of them myself, but how does it "break"? This other person that came in your life did not bring a part of your heart with them and later took it away, No. Neither did they hammer yours while leaving, then how does it break? Maybe it is not the heart that breaks, but rather the soul that does. The void you feel after a true love lost is created in your soul, and it is the heart that takes all the blame.

Humans have exhausted their ability to rely on themselves. Despite centuries of fighting battles using nothing but their bodies and their own mind, they have lost all of it. Humans now mostly rely on other human beings to do their work. Only a small percentage of the world population still "prefers" using their legs for transport, whereas other use vehicles. This is a little example, but worth realizing.

What is the nature of pain? It certainly comes to all of us and every time, it stings you a little differently every time. It always stings in a way that it produces a newer torture in your bones whenever it comes. We sure learn from it, but does everyone? Is everyone that powerful? Certainly they are not. And so pain heals some, but drowns others.

We all have different paths. All of us are unique and go our separate ways but why is it that we love this small little time when we are together? Why is it that we miss this time spent in togetherness? Certainly this special time is missed because it contains nothing but love. Love of ourselves among “our people”.

Freedom is usually seen as the liberation from something in the physical sense. You think you are “free” from your past mistakes, or you are free tomorrow to meet a friend but, it is more of from the mind than is in the physical aspect. Breaking away from things like generational trauma or forgiving yourself for example, needs you to achieve freedom yes, but of the mind.

Comfort and luxury go side by side but what is the fundamental definition of comfort? Is it the same for everyone? Certainly not. Comfort to you may mean a bigger bed or a faster internet but to a single mother for example, it only means providing everything for her child and seeing her cheer up. Comfort is simple, but it is subjective.

Your Mind is such a beautiful place, have you noticed? It takes you everywhere in an instant. Be it your favorite memory of a friend or your favorite destination. You close your eyes and open your “mind’s eye” to teleport yourself to somewhere special. Your mind does everything in its power to make you physically feel that you are there. But, it is always such a wonderful place? Definitely not. Can you still choose to make it beautiful? Definitely yes.

You may think as to why do people always seem to be in a hurry. You may even know someone who is always in a hurry despite them not being the busiest person you know, but they still seem to steal the least time in reaching somewhere. You see, people always have reasons. The people that always live a fast paced life seem to be that way because they want to make time for the place they are going to, or they understand that the place they need to go requires them to be there at the earliest.

Fears are scary but they are beautiful. The strongest of people have already formed countless philosophies around them. You see, without fear you would always saying a big yes to all the things coming your way, even if they end in your downfall later down the line. It is the fear that grows big enough to help you dodge certain situations so you can say yes to the correct ones.

Joy is the very soul of everything you do. It is the ring of your heart, the bell of it which announces that happiness has arrived. What good is life without the joy of small things? Your favorite coffee. Your bestest friend. Your happy place and your most thrilling movie. All of this mean nothing if joy were to meet extinction. I wonder, though, as we age why do we stop meeting with joy? Why do we let it die?

What is the color of life? Does it have one? Certainly the things that make things special have color. The color of peace seems to be blue whereas the color of love is red.

Yellow is the color of youth and Green the color of freshness. What but, is the color of us? Is it the mixture of all of these that makes us all choose our favorite colors? Perhaps our color is more vibrant, maybe a rainbow.

Death comes to all that is for certain, but beware. There is death that takes away your body and your breath and then there is death that takes your soul away. The former we cannot choose to delay, for it is certain. The latter however somehow in our conscious control and it does not take many people go further once they have encountered the latter. The former is silent and ends instantly, but the latter? It takes away pieces of you away in the forms of excruciating pains until there is nothing left to live for. I pray however, if you meet the latter, may you only allow it to destroy you for love and only love. Nothing more and nothing less.

Poetries are written and they are spoken. But it is sometimes not the words that matter but rather who is it made for. The person listening to it sometimes makes all the difference in the world. Poetries are unique and that is in the sense that all of us have one inside each of us. All we are searching is someone who is skilled enough to hear them from us.

And remember, money is only a tool. You use it too much; you become a puppet yourself without you realizing it in the process. When you do realize it, it is all too late and your loved ones and you yourself are too far to reach by then.

You are only as good as your best people. Remember, to be happy you need not be with them in order to be happy, you only need another dive in the memories that involve them. Maybe even make or recreate the best ones!

The true wisdom of a wise man is not in understanding what brings happiness into this world, but rather to understand what brings and causes the peak of the most gut wrenching pains for it is in the latter that he shall find the most answers to the first question he is looking to solve.

And what I have noticed is that we may think that patience and the power of will are two different things, but no. They are only different words, synonyms for each other which mean the same thing.

Legacy you see, it is such a beautiful thing. While some people leave big money and even bigger companies as their legacies behind, it is also worth noting that even something as little as your unending kindness towards everyone you meet can be your biggest legacy. To also realize on your death bed that even if you earned a little less money in life, you still earned a lot of hearts.

We all know for the most parts that early humans created manuscripts and alphabets but, have you ever wondered how were books created? How did someone come up with the idea that you can contain a whole new world amidst two words and ten. You can step into a completely new world with only reading what is written. Books are magic indeed.

Time is for sure limited and conversely and ironically unlimited. For a fool who is purpose-less and has no goal, time is unlimited and even entertaining. But for the wise who knows that they were sent here to pray and focus on a singular mission which is planted uniquely inside their heart, they know it is limited. Time for sure is something beautiful, moving through us and around us without us even feeling the tinge of it. Time is similar to air.

Healed people you see, glow differently. They sit among you but when they smile, it makes your heart smile. Not just your outer self, but your heart. They walk differently and light up everyone around them. Everyone has light but you see, Healed people are the ones who bring out that light.

Kindness is perceived as a gift by most people, but it is not. It is a quality and this is not something that is learned. Kindness comes from conscience. The very conscience that makes you and I human. So, kindness is inborn. All you have to do is wear it. But certainly as is with humans, most of them are rather lazy with their wardrobe choices.

Think about a life without purpose. To be born, learn the ways of human kind, and still to simply exist. To go through the ways of life and dread through, from one day to the next without anything pushing you forward. But that is the lesson. To make life worthwhile by dedicating every living breath to a mission. May it be love, life or something greater. That is what a purpose is worth.

How clever is Satan, using nothing but the weakest of whispers to produce some of the strongest of temptations. And alas! how weak are we the mortals. Following all these little voices in our heads, calling it sometimes laziness and sometimes our comfort. Not realizing that these words are also already the children of Satan himself.

And I would love you not for the longest of times but for the longest of breaths. For it will not be just forevers and centuries but I will be holding on to this love from the first breath that I saw you till the final breath that you and I take. Until then, you are my home always.

-----------------The End ---------------

Printed by Libri Plureos GmbH in Hamburg, Germany